Wandering Wisely

In Balance

Rita Makkannaw

WANDERING WISELY
In Balance

Copyright © Rita Makkannaw, 2025

All rights reserved. No part of this publication may be reproduced, stored in a retrieval system, or transmitted in any form or by any means, electronic, mechanical, photocopying, recording, or otherwise, without written permission of the author and publisher.

Published by Rita Makkannaw, Edmonton, Canada

ISBN:
    Paperback   978-1-77354-727-5
        ebook   978-1-77354-736-7

Publication assistance by

PageMaster.ca

This is not a perfect book because I did not aim for perfection. Had I aimed for perfection, I would be guaranteed to fail. I aimed for humanness. Nothing artificial here. Except I did use spellcheck.

Acknowledgements

I would like to give special acknowledgment to three people who read through the manuscript. Morningstar Mercredi, Carlo Marazzo and Lesa Yule all made invaluable contributions, like getting rid of some unnecessary adjectives and making suggestions to improve wording here and there. A special thanks to Morningstar for her description of this book for the back cover. I would also like to acknowledge Jan Redsted for the star design and all of his help with my previous publications.

I would also like to acknowledge the numerous Elders from Australia, Europe and all over Turtle Island (North America) who were my teachers. A special recognition to my late husband Raven Makkannaw, whose love and patience in his teachings was a wonder to behold.

Hai Hai. Ish Nish, Mahsi Cho, Merci Beaucoup, Tak and Thank you.

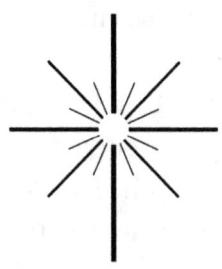

Foreward

My journey of understanding of spirituality and connectedness began in 1983. I have said I was hit over the head with a spiritual baseball bat. Many things happened that were a mystery to me. After a grueling three-year search, contacting numerous people who might be able to help me unravel the mystery of my visions and experiences. I had no luck until I met Raven Makkannaw, a Cree wisdom keeper and elder from Muskwacis Alberta. He not only had answers, but it was the start of true love that resulted in a long marriage.

In our travels together I learned much from extraordinary people of great spiritual knowledge, which I knew nothing about because I never paid attention even though it was there all along.

The forty years I spent sitting with traditional wisdom keepers has been a precious gift. Some call the people who have not lost their traditional knowledge taught over countless generations, 'nature people'.

They are people to whom were passed the seven laws of Honour, Love, Honesty, Courage, Humility, Wisdom, and Truth which are guiding principles for a good earth journey. They are people who have not lost the wisdom of connectedness to all nature or an understanding of spirituality and how to nourish our soul. They are people who know how to live life through connectedness, ritual, ceremony, humour and just living life the best way possible as it unfolds. Wisdom keepers come in all colors, all nationalities, all genders, or a cross of any of the above. They have great teachings which could be a guiding light for making the world a better place for all the living beings with which we share space. We just need to listen.

I mostly lived in silence for seven years after Raven and I got together, because when the elders spoke, I heard their words and I knew in my heart they were true, but often I did not fully understand what they meant. When they spoke about spirit I did not understand, when they spoke about how things were unfolding the way the Creator meant them to be, I did not understand. I only knew that Raven loved me, and I loved him, and I couldn't possibly deny my own truth. I became painfully aware of just how little I knew at a time when I thought I knew lots.

This book is not about our differences in methods of connectedness, but of the connectedness itself and how we are all spiritual beings. Spiritual knowledge is spiritual knowledge no matter who you are or where you live or your belief system.

This book is not about my story either because everyone has a different life journey and mine is no more or less important than yours or anyone else's.

It is a sharing of spiritual knowledge and understanding I learned from Elders of how to use all of ourselves, to become as strong and happy as possible. This book is a sharing of how I became aware of my spirituality within and outside of myself. It is about a personal recognition of how much I learned to walk in my own shoes. As I learn the one thing that has happenned is that the more I know, the more I know I don't know.

I decided to share some of the teachings that are the foundation of connectedness with self for all people. Everyone can go on a journey to find their own path to a life of harmony.

I originally wrote in first person, however I decided to share anecdotes of lessons learned that are universal to all people. We all share a commonness which may be expressed in different ways, but has the same spiritual foundation. We are here for an earth journey and when our body stops functioning, we go home to the spirit world. Raven took his journey home in 2011.

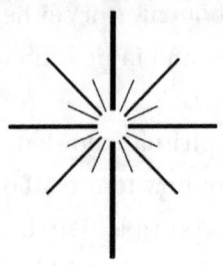

CHAPTER 1

The Star

We are all stars that shine in our own light.
We are the center of our own universe.

The star came to me during a very brief prayer when I did not know what to tell a lady who had come to me for advice about spirituality.

I had recently gone back to my home country of Denmark, after I lost Raven. My cousins, where I was staying, had a teepee pitched in their back yard where the lady and I retreated to talk. I was not sure how I could help her, but I thought I could at least hear her out. She had recently been to a workshop presented by a native person. He gave a circle teaching about the four main elements of ourselves.

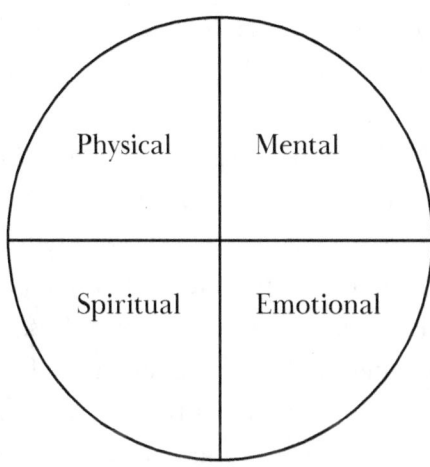

His teachings were very meaningful, going into all aspects of us as humans. These teachings have been used with great success for thousands of people in understanding ourselves, but as with any teachings it does not always work for every person all the time. This lady was totally wrought because she felt she knew nothing about her spiritual self, so her wheel went kerplunk- kerplunk as it turned. I became very quiet and said silently. "Creator, please help me with this one. I just don't know where I can go from here"

As I sat there, I began drawing. First the cross and I asked her what that meant to her. She said it could be four directions or the physical, mental, emotional and spiritual. Then I began to fill in the other lines in between. Then suddenly the words came that explained how we were all a shining star. All aspects of ourselves are connected to the core of WHO we are, each affecting the other. There are also aspects that fall in between these four categories. She felt much better seeing herself as a star. I knew I had received help. It was not from me. I said a quick thank you before leaving the teepee. Then I remembered a time when I could not even imagine the use of prayer and I became emotionally overwhelmed with gratitude for all the things I had learned.

I realized that the star is a great representation of WHO we are as individual humans. We all shine in our own way. Each vertical and horizontal axis represents our four elements. The physical, the mental, the spiritual, and the emotional, all come together in the center as the core of ourselves. We are a combination of all, and we shine in all directions from our center. Sometimes more in the mental, like when we study. Sometimes the emotional like when we are in a state of heightened happiness or sadness, sometimes in the physical when we train our bodies to become stronger or faster, sometimes in the spiritual like when we pray, or just sit in gratitude or in a peaceful place where we appreciate ourselves, and those around us, including all that is in nature. Everyone is a star that shines in its own light, as we share space, with all that inhabit our world.

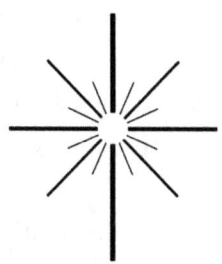

CHAPTER 2

What is spirituality?

Our spirit holds our reverence

Your spirit is that part of yourself that holds reverence. We all possess spirit. If the spirit leaves, our bodies stop functioning. No spirit, no life as we know it in physical form. Spirit is an energy and according to science, energy can neither be created or destroyed, therefore, it must go somewhere.

Spirit holds knowledge which is different from brain knowledge. Sometimes I just call it magic, because we cannot explain it but it is real. Of that there is no doubt. Scientists are constantly 'discovering' about the spiritual energy connection between plants, animals and people. Nature people have known these things since time immemorial, but western science needs to prove everything in their own way. The problem with that method is that not all aspects of spirituality can be proven using scientific methodology. It is what it is.

Our spirit is what connects our soul with all that is in our world, be they two legged, four legged, flying, swimming or standing still. It is you individually becoming a part of a collective on a heart level. Your spirituality is your truth, your connectedness, and your feelings. Spirituality has its home in the heart the same way the mental has its home in the brain, but the heart or spirit has to be moved before your brain can process your desires. If your spirit does not move you to do something, you won't. According to elders' teachings, your spirit is connecting you to the outside, the soul is that space deep inside that's your private place in the solidity of you. They are not disconnected as you experience life in balance.

Spirit lives beyond ones physical and so you may feel the spirit of a perfect stranger you have come in contact with. Maybe in an elevator, or the grocery store. If their spirit is not comfortable for you, that is ok. Maybe your spirit is not within their comfort zone either. In any case, you can remove yourself without judgement, without figuring out why. Just accept that it is what it is. Sometimes when someone walks into a room, you instantly feel good in their presence, so if spending time with that person is enjoyable, do it. If on the other hand the opposite is true, remove yourself, or them if possible. You can also protect yourself by filling your thoughts with things that do not involve the other person or simply ignore them. Some people will use various techniques like surrounding themselves with a white light, or setting up an imaginary shield between themselves and the person or people that make them uncomfortable. There are many techniques, and the more you seek the more examples you will find. Just pick the ones that work for you.

Different people have different beliefs. Maybe they are all right.

Unfortunately, or fortunately, we are not privy to understanding exactly what happens after our spirit leaves our body. Native people understand we are on an earth journey and when our spirit leaves, we go home.

Millions of people have a connection in one way or the other with their ancestors so there must be something to it. I wonder if it does not happen to everyone. Some, like me before I met 'Nature People' did not pay attention. Some people believe it cannot be true. It is what it is for each of us.

The wisdom keepers knew that everyone has spiritual intelligence.

They could connect with those who entered their space and those who intended to enter their space. They see people, not only with their eyes, but with their spirit and soul. Raven often knew when someone was coming for help with a certain ailment, and he would be prepared by the time they arrived. Some people are gifted to know, just as others have other gifts.

Some people might call the connectedness insight or intuition or even a gut feeling. When your gut gives you a hunch about something present or future pay attention. That feeling did not come for no reason.

Trusting your gut feelings or intuition, is one aspect of staying true to yourself.

When someone talks about the heart being moved, others will say the spirit or soul is moved. It is all the same. The words are not important. The definitions are not important. Your feelings and experiences are.

You can never truly know someone else's spiritual feelings. You only know your own. When someone says "I know how you feel" it is impossible. You know how you feel under the same circumstances. No one's feelings are wrong. We all have our own spiritual truth and our truth is ours. As we evolve through life, we are exposed to new concepts, some of which we will keep and others we will discard. The only constant in life is change. That is why Elders carry so much wisdom. They have lived through many changes which has given them an understanding of humanity some people long to know.

Many of us have grown up in a society where we were asked "What were you thinking?" How many times are you asked, "What were you feeling?" Many grew up without guidance about spirit. Some people who joined an organized religion are left with the impression that the heads of their organization are the ones who have all the knowledge. No one is dependent on a leader for their own spiritual wellbeing, but they can be of great help to understand ourselves better. Just be cautious about giving away your own spiritual power to someone else. Not taking responsibility for your own spiritual journey will be detrimental to your own wellbeing.

Only you can know yourself. That does not mean there is a need to avoid organized religions. It means that if a particular faith group fits well with your spirit and you find a good spiritual community, it is good.

Spiritual understanding of self and connectedness with all is something the 'Nature' people around the world know, but often you will hear them say "I know nothing." They understand that they cannot fully know another person and so all they can do is share their knowledge and you need to decide for yourself what is yours. Chances are their sharing may be invaluable. Know that your road to learning is never ending. Is that not of great comfort?

One interesting observation is that some people deny knowing these things, but they still use their free-thinking spiritual knowledge.

Many people use the term spirit in their everyday language without giving it much thought such as 'team spirit', 'I just don't have the spirit for it.' 'He or she is mean spirited.' 'He or she has a kind spirit.' 'Spirit in our workplace is good or bad." Whether we think about the meaning or not, we still use these terms, and we have an understanding of what they mean.

Spirit is real and almost everyone honors it in one way or the other. Some through organised religion or some through being alone in nature. Some find solace in praying alone, some in praying with others. Some in just being aware. Those who pay attention greatly enrich their lives.

Some people have questioned whether the people who do evil things have a soul. They do or they would be dead. Unfortunately, some people use their soul in an evil way. Some are takers of souls, meaning they have learned how to manipulate their believers in any way they wish. Be careful not to give up your ability to be a free thinker. People who live good lives and do not do evil things cannot for the most part understand the thinking of evil. Some people have been known to follow evil to the point of administering their children poison and then taking poison themselves. When people stop blindly following someone else wisdom keepers say that they have taken their spirits back and became the people they were meant to be. Having the spiritual strength to stick to your values and not taking on someone else's is of great benefit. You can keep your own values without giving your spiritual self to someone else.

Certain people came to our home and told Raven all about their strong spiritual beliefs. Sometimes what they expressed did not make sense, even for me and I didn't know much at all. I would be confused when Raven just let them ramble on and say nothing. I questioned that after they left. He would just say "you cannot tell anyone anything that knows it all". It's a good motto to live by as you just waste your time trying to convince someone of something if their mind is strongly made up. Certain people will never be free thinkers. We may all believe differently, but if we close our minds and hearts to learning new things, we won't. If we don't want to learn or believe new things that is ok. Seek what you have a desire to learn.

It is possible to leave a part of your spirit somewhere else. Most common is an acute case of homesickness. When you cannot get home out of your mind, and you go a little crazy until you go back home, you know you are homesick.

Sometimes when people move, they may have a profound loneliness for the place they left behind, even if mentally they know the move was for the best. A part of yourself can also be left with another person that you may have loved, but you are no longer together. There are many reasons. The most important thing is to always take all of yourself with you wherever you go. Be fully present in the moment, no matter where you go or what you do.

One woman came to us because she felt so disjointed. Sometimes she would suddenly see herself as a jigsaw puzzle that was not put together. When it was explained to her how she had left pieces of her spirit at all her past places, it was like a light was lit and she knew what she had to do. Because she didn't have her own traditional ceremonies, she just followed her heart and one day gathered something from each place she had left her spirit. She put everything in a pail, took it out in the wilderness and had a burning and prayed for help to gather herself together again. She was invited to come for a sweat lodge for help. She came, but she had already done the work herself.

Some people who have been incarcerated for a long period of time may leave a part of their spirit behind. Then they will go back behind bars as they will need to bring all of themselves together. It can also happen when a person is tortured. When they come back and are zombie like, they too may need to have help to call their spirit back. Those who do not understand may mistake it for post-traumatic stress disorder. It could be one or the other or both.

There have been other instances of this, and people have either called their own spirit back or went to wisdom keepers for help. In any case, wherever you travel, however you live your life, live it in the present. Take all of yourself with you wherever you may go.

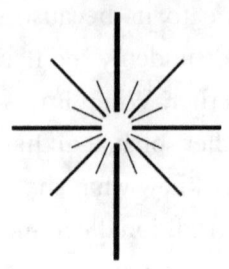

CHAPTER 3

Be Who You Are

You are born perfect why change perfection? Everyone is an important piece in the puzzle of humanity.

One of the most basic teachings of all the wisdom keepers is to BE WHO YOU ARE. What does that mean? When they said that we are all born perfect just the way we are was confusing. I was very aware of people born with challenges. How could that be perfect? I was to learn that they are all our teachers.

I was a white woman in the Native world, and that was not always something I could be proud of because of what happened at the hands of my people. I was just starting to learn about those atrocities. Their truth made me physically ill. It was Elders who came to my rescue and helped me see the reality of the situation. Just because we did not individually do harm, I think we do have a collective responsibility for what happened. Educating ourselves with truth is helpful.

Most people struggle with how to live their best life. The partnership of head and heart is most powerful. When the elders spoke about the fact that "the journey from your head to your heart is the longest journey you will ever take" was something else I never understood, until I did. I knew how to use my head very well, but with the spiritual side of myself, I was not so confident. That was the beginning of a long, painful journey of learning. When I discovered who I was individually it became much easier to live with the truth of what is.

My spiritual journey actually began before I met Raven. Many strange experiences which I did not understand had happened. One day I had a profound urge to attend a Therapeutic Touch workshop at Grant McEwan College in Edmonton. We all sat in a circle and the first exercise was a centering exercise. That began by relaxing each part of our body beginning with the toes and working our way up to the top of our heads. Then we were to think about a place and a time when we felt happy and healthy. It could be running as a child, sitting in nature, a wedding, anytime, anywhere. We were given the time to find our time and place. Then we were told to pay attention to the feeling of happiness and healthiness. The next step was to bring that feeling to all the parts of our body. After some time, we were told to bring the feeling to our circle, then to our community, then to our province, then to the north pole and the south pole. Then bring that feeling all the way around the world. After some time of remaining in that space the instructor began reversing the process, stopping when we were holding the positive space between head and heart. After some time of holding that space, she brought us to the awareness of the circle we occupied. Then we began sharing where we had gone, what space we had found. Some went to a space of a relationship with a loved one, a time of running as a child, alone or with someone else. Some went to a time when they connected in a profound way to a place and time in nature. Some women went to the birth of a child. Everyone went to a place and time where connectedness with others or nature was involved. No one went to their place of employment. After sharing we were told that where we went had no relevance to the exercise anyway. What was relevant was the feeling we had in the connectedness of head and heart. The feeling we had was our most powerful place for reverence, for protection from the negative we may encounter, and for a place where we could make our best decisions. At that moment I became aware of what the wisdom keepers meant with the phrase of 'be WHO you are.

You are the only expert on yourself. Everyone and everything around you may be your helpers. There are times we need all the help we can get. But we are in fact in charge of our own destiny. This is just another tool in your toolbox of wisdom. Knowledge comes in many different forms. Mental intelligence is all about facts and figures. Decisions made by the brain are generally logical but sometimes the logic of the brain may interfere with intuition, or spiritual knowledge. There is space for both. The brain and the heart make a most powerful team.

Being true to ourselves is a gift. We can be open to the possibilities of other's truth, but until we know something to be true for ourselves, it is not for us. You can acknowledge the wisdom, or gift of someone else's truth, even when you cannot agree with their concepts. We all have our own truths about ourselves. We are the center of our own universe. We all have endless possibilities but only within our own truth. If you can sing opera and your spirit is happy, sing. If you can't, why waste your time and effort even trying? You can just enjoy someone else's talents. You have your own. Exploring and finding what makes your spirit happy, is what is most important. That will give you peace in your heart. Your spirit will be more at rest and chances are you may even sleep better at night.

No one's truth remains the same their whole life, because as we journey we are exposed to new wisdom and new ideas. Change is the only constant which is always with us. Sometimes we have to close doors, but when one door closes another will open. Take the good things from your past with you and discard whatever does not serve a purpose in the present. Your truth in the moment is what's important.

To use all of WHO you are in order to become all you are meant to be means we should question everything we see and hear. Question ourselves, with an open mind and without judgement. Keep what suits your heart and mind, let the rest go. Then you live your own journey.

Exploring is a wonderful space where we examine what is right for us and what we need to change.

A dear friend of mine in his seventies struggled much of his life to figure out why, in the core of himself his spirit was troubled, even though he lived a good productive life.

In a series of dreams, he heard the call of his spirit which manifested more as a woman than the man he physically was. In his seventies he decided to pursue a transsexual path to be who she really is as a woman. Once she made the decision, she told her wife who immediately lent her support for his decision. My friend still had great concerns about telling her family. As it turned out needlessly so. Their reaction ranged from cool, to concern about the surgery. Not one member questioned her decision nor turned her away. It is never too late to come to a place of peace and honesty in the core of who we are.

That means using all of yourself to figure out your path. What others think should have no bearing. It is yours and yours alone. Following your destiny may make life difficult for the people in your circle. That is their issue. They need to handle their lives for themselves. Supporting people to move freely into the space where they need to be at any one time creates harmony. Your life, no matter how difficult a path you choose will have its rewards when you are true to yourself, often beyond what even you can imagine. Be your own best friend.

Our core peace is what is most important not only for us, but for all those in our circle, our community and for the world.

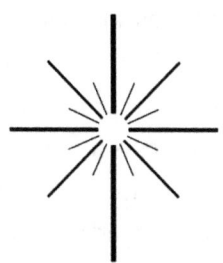

CHAPTER 4

Allowing Children to be Who They Are

Children and old people are closest to the Creator.

Children are our best teachers, until they 'lose their innocence' as the elders would say, or until they develop filters. Their honesty is a treasure to behold. Their reaction to their surroundings should never be ignored. They possess an instinct only the innocents have.

Traditional teachings of the Native people are 'never yell at a child. It hurts their spirit' When a child does something wrong, as all children do, they need to be taught, not punished.

This can be done gently as well as effectively. The willow is considered the teaching plant in many cultures. Native people use it for teaching, not for punishment. A friend who was always getting into trouble as a child had to be taught many times. Her father made her take tobacco to a willow bush and pray for guidance to understand what she had done wrong and then she was to cut a branch and bring it to her father. He put the willow branch on the table while he spoke. He never used it on her. There was no need. She listened.

When physical punishment is used, the child is taught to use physical punishment to accomplish what they want. Not a good teaching. Think about how you would like to be treated when you are taught. No one wants to be assaulted.

Children do need guidance as they figure out their space in the world. As much as possible let them make their own mistakes as lessons are best remembered from experience. For instance, if a child does not want to put on a coat to go outside in the middle of winter let them go. They will soon discover the consequences of their decision and scurry back in the house for a coat. That gives you the opportunity to praise them for figuring it out on their own. Allowing a child to make their own decisions as much as possible gives them the skills needed as an adult to evaluate consequences of the decisions they make. Getting hurt a little will allow them to learn where to set their own limits. They need the freedom to figure out consequences as long as their decisions do not have dire consequences. Always remember to praise a child whenever appropriate. Actions such as a pat on the head or a thumbs up for something well done helps a child's confidence. So does "atta boy" or "atta girl." Children are not hard to please. You can do so many things like when you make pancakes design them like animals. Maybe they can guess which animal it is. They are always right of course. A picnic, even in your home can be fun. Time at the playground and so much more.

Don't worry if your child throws a temper tantrum. Maybe that's their way of letting go of negative energy. Children do not always have the words needed to articulate their feelings so they may be expressing themselves physically in which case it will pass. They may also be doing it for attention, in which case it is most important not to reward bad behaviour. It will soon stop and they will try something else. If it is a good thing, which it most likely will be, make sure to give the child your undivided attention and praise them for their good behaviour. You can help your child's spirit so they can tackle life from a place of strength.

Children react the same way adults do to many words. No one likes to be told to do something NOW. We, as adults like to have preparation time. They do too. Give them that same respect. Another word to avoid as much as possible is NO. No one likes to be told no. With the right questions they will most often come to the decision you want them to come to. With an explanation why it's not a good idea to eat junk food before dinner works much better than saying no, period. Because I said so is not good enough. You have your reasons for saying no, just explain.

Another way to bolster them spiritually is by giving them choices. One choice may not be good for them, give them options so when they choose what they want, praise them for their good thinking. Kids will be kids. They don't always listen to mom and dad. When children were difficult in the traditional Native community the parents would bring gifts to the elders and their child would have to sit with them for a teaching. That could be for a short time or a long time. You can utilize your own choice of elders in your family or amongst your friends to do the same.

Teaching your child that what is, is, and that's important. If you are not first in a race, you are not first. As simple as that. You are where you are, you are who you are. There is never any purpose in comparing. Additionally, children only competed against themselves, just working to be better than before.

Relax, have fun, and love them and you have done a great job, the rest is up to them. The quantity of your time is not nearly as important as the quality. That means keeping phone calls and other distractions to a minimum in their presence.

All you can do is give a child the freedom and ability to be who they are meant to be, not who you think they should be. No matter what others say. Being aware of your child's wellbeing spiritually is important. If you make a mistake, your child's reaction should teach you something. Just know that you did the best you knew how in the moment and figure out a way of making things right between you. That means creating a teaching for the child which he or she understands.

Another interesting observation was when we developed the Healthy Babies program for Capital Health. We called together mothers who were interested in doing their best for their children. Many had been gutter drunks and drug addicted and was now on a road to recovery. One thing they had in common was that they loved their children, even through all their challenges. They loved them the best they could at the time.

Often in life people who live with incredibly difficult challenges still love the best they can, and no one can do more. We included the mothers as much as possible in the decision of who would take care of their child if they could not. Being a part of making the best decisions for their child allowed them the satisfaction of knowing their child was in good hands. It was often good for the children when they got older and understood more. Allowing your child to grow up in a good home where it's spirit is allowed to soar, and fall, is a wonderful gift to the world.

Guiding a child through it's formative years, is indeed both a gift and a challenge. Does anything work all the time on everybody? Absolutely not. Are there any guarantees of success in raising a child? Never. In any case, when they become adults, some will do well, others won't. It is what it is. Never stop loving. Live life as you need to do for yourself. Do not allow others to influence you out of your heartfelt needs. Every person makes choices for their life and they and only they, as adults are responsible for the choices they make. All anyone can do is their best. Provide the tools they need. If they use them, great. If they don't, that's on them. As adults they are responsible for their behaviour. Raising a child to be a productive and happy human being who lives life on their own terms is indeed a gift to the world.

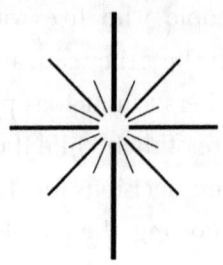

CHAPTER 5

Sacred Space

Doing nothing is doing lots

Finding a place which feels good for you and only you, or those you invite in can be most helpful on your journey. A place that is magical for you. It can be a corner in your house, a place in your back yard, a place by a river or in a park, or in a forest. It can be anywhere. The place you choose has but one goal. It feels good in your heart. A place where you can feel a connectedness with your own spirit, with your own magic. A place where you can search your own mind, and ask your spirit for guidance to help you.

It is a place where you can do ceremony all by yourself or with someone. Spirit loves ceremony. One woman who lived way up north in a very crowded house said that she sometimes went into the bathroom, locked the door and said her prayers. Some people find it in a good bath, so even the bathroom can be a sacred place. Any place that works for you is good.

If you like, you can smudge, which means lighting something to create a smoke which brings peace to your soul. It could be incense or the like. Whatever works for you. Native people use different herbs including tobacco, sweetgrass, sage and cedar. You can find many types of herbs in stores and in nature. Find the one that makes your spirit happy. The important thing is to search for whatever suits you best. You can also bring a little food if you wish. Just remember to give thanks because you have it and can enjoy it. Consuming food that makes your mouth water will strengthen your soul. To others it may seem like you are doing nothing, doing nothing might be doing lots. It can be the most important thing you will ever do.

There is a very simple ceremony anyone can do in that place. It is to breathe. Breathing is the simplest ceremony there is. Breathe conscientiously, slowly and deeply, paying attention to every breath. That will not only bring many good things you need to your physical body, but it will affect your spiritual body. It will help bring emotional trauma to a manageable place.

Breathing deep with concentration on your breath can give you a break from thinking about other things and allow you to go to a sacred space where nothing matters except your breathing. Every aspect of yourself is integrated to prepare your heart to receive whatever you are seeking.

After a while you can stop and pay attention to all the little things within your sacred space. If you are outdoors, you will find it alive with all kinds of beings. The birds, trees, and the little wildlife, like bugs and insects all become a part of your world in the quietness of your sacred space.

Giving thanks for all the beauty which has entered your life in your present moment is another simple ceremony. Fire can be very beneficial, even a candle. Watch how the flame dances and brings light to you. You can also chant or sing for a bit. Spirit loves that too. Almost every organized religion uses song or chanting. Whether alone or with others, it is good for the soul. Even a short break from being overwhelmed with a current challenging situation is a good rest. Anything that gives you just a little relief for a little while is perfect. After you take a break, no matter how brief, it becomes easier to handle whatever is troubling you. Spend time thinking about possibilities for your future. The past cannot be changed, but when you bring the possibilities of the future into your heart, you can go on a good life journey. When you reach that point you become much stronger to move on in a good way. Just have patience with yourself as it may take longer than you would like.

Before you leave your sacred place, it is always good to go with thankfulness in your heart for the moments of your sacred experience. Be thankful to those who have helped you both from the spirit world and your physical world.

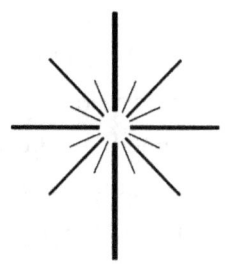

CHAPTER 6

Ritual and Ceremony

Whichever ritual or ceremony that is good for your soul is good

Any ritual or ceremony that makes your heart feel good is good. It does not have to be the same as anyone else's. If you do not have a tradition, make one.

Ceremonies have many purposes. They may be a celebration of all that is good in your world in the moment. They are also gatherings for thankfulness and for asking for guidance for your future, or for healing. They may be a collective gathering or done in solitude. Words can be very valuable or not necessary. Honouring your own spirit is the essence of your purpose.

How you do ceremony varies depending on what your tradition teaches. They are done at Christmas, Thanksgiving and even Halloween. Some people have elaborate celebrations of good over evil, some have special ways of celebrating birthdays or anniversaries and funerals. Some are for the change of the guard at palaces, some for a coronation. In any case we are surrounded by ceremony.

Traditional tribes have sacred ceremonies for all things that happen in nature. Of gratefulness to the Creator and Mother Earth, of solstices and equinoxes as they signify the passing of the seasons and for the right time to harvest medicines and food. They have ceremonies for the coming of a little one to this earth, and for leaving it again. Ceremonies of gratefulness for all the things that sustain us. They are all the same, only different. Although cultures across the world have different and often intricate ceremonies, the foundational purpose of these ceremonies is to help or to expand one's spiritual knowledge, and to give thanks or ask for guidance, among others.

Ceremonies are very helpful both for you and those who you support. Utilizing the simple ceremonies such as smudging and breathing is good. Never allow communities to make a judgement on what is good for you. Only you know that, so follow your own heart, your own feelings, no matter what others think or say.

Prayer with other people allows you to feel the collective sacred energy with others. Finding your faith community can be a wonderful thing, but not necessary for your own spiritual health. Who we feel compatible with comes down to our own feelings. Therefore, no judgement of right or wrong. There are only differences. Pick who and what is good for you and leave the rest alone. It is what it is.

Ritual differs from ceremony. It is something you consciously do the same way all the time just because it makes you feel good. One young man told me in no uncertain terms that he was not a believer in such things. He had a very strong soul connection to nature, especially stones. I asked him how he began his mornings. He told me that he liked to wake up before his wife, make a good pot of coffee and go sit under a certain tree and enjoy the peaceful morning. That is ritual. Doing the same thing over and over because it makes you feel good. Feeling good in the moment is the point of ritual. Some people have created ritual out of brushing their teeth, having a bath, running or walking. It doesn't matter what we do or when we do it. Choose what's right for you. The important thing is to be aware of how doing certain little things makes you feel good and then do them. Nourishment for the soul. Why not explore? It can't hurt.

In any case ceremony and ritual must be important for our wellbeing as they are done one way or the other all over the world by both humans and animals.

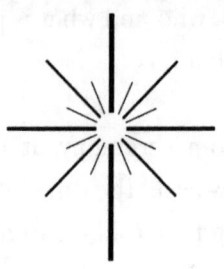

CHAPTER 7

When your Heart or Spirit is Broken

You are WHO you are, not your brokenness

When your heart has been broken, it is broken. Mourning someone or something is a broken spirit which will need healing. The healing process takes whatever time it takes to heal.

An abusive relationship damages your spirit. That can be with a partner, a sibling, a parent, an adult child or close friend. When it is recognized as such and you remove yourself from the situation, a successful healing journey can begin. One thing that may be helpful is to tell yourself all the things you would tell your best friend were they in your situation. Doing it out loud may be even better. Hearing your own words and good advice to your friend may help to have a fresh look at your situation and bring clarity to your path forward.

Sometimes trauma can be carried from one generation to another. Some people call it past lives memory. Native people say it is blood memory. In any case the trauma is real and needs to be dealt with if it is felt in the present. There are many ways this can be done. Some solutions you may find yourself. Like becoming aware of what is from the past and what is from your present. Our feelings will rise to the surface before your reasoning cuts in. If you can take a moment and ask yourself if your feelings have roots in the past or if it is really a current issue, you may become aware that it is from your past. If so, do some self talk before you unwittingly take your feelings out on someone who has done nothing wrong. Seek out whatever sources may help.

Look for those who may be your helpers. Talking to a trained professional who has studied your particular problem may help, especially if you do not have clarity on the scope of your issues. Talking to a friend might help, talking to your grandmother or grandfather may help you find the path to peace you seek. Going for a long walk or run might be good. Playing your favorite music might give you a lift, as may drumming. Being aware of what brings your spirit along on a healing path is good. Being grateful for any progress made is very healing. Seeking out your own path to alleviate the difficult challenges you face is your gift to yourself and those around you. In any case it is your journey.

Sometimes you may feel very tired, as if you have lost all your strength. You may have. In that case there are many ways to retrieve it. Extensive rest and sleep may help, but if someone calls and wants you to do something together that you love to do, go and enjoy yourself if you can.

Make a small to do list that you know you can accomplish without too much stress. Aim to have a good day today, but if a day is too long, make it an hour, and if that is too long just have a good minute. Plan to make every moment of your life the best you can. Keep in mind that you also need to take time to cry. Crying is a wonderful tool for healing. We feel better after having a good cry. What's wrong with that? Ignore what you may have been taught in your past and just let it out. Honour your feelings and don't judge them. Just look after your needs as they arise.

Never put clothes on your body you don't like. Wear what suits you. In the meantime, do not forget to be grateful. There are so many things we can be grateful for. Your favorite piece of clothing, the food that makes your mouth water, having a bed to sleep on, the sun, the moon, the change of the seasons and on and on and on. Even the homeless have expressed gratitude for what little they have. They have community. Many have a great sense of humour. That's a gift.

There are other helpers too. All plants including trees have their own unique energy which they can share with you if you ask. If you put your hands a couple of centimeters from the tree you will likely feel an energy surrounding it. It too has an energy which is bigger than the physical. Try several and be conscious of the one that feels best for you. You can stand or sit up against it and ask the tree to share its energy. The exchange may be so subtle that you may not even notice at first, but if you just remain in your most comfortable position for a period of time, you will feel the sharing. The earth is another powerful source of energy. You can stand up, best in bare feet or lie down. Don't forget that you have four sides.

In any case, you do want to stay in balance.

Finding an isolated place and shouting out your misery can be helpful. Being thankful is wonderfully beneficial as well. The moments you can spend being thankful are moments of peace for your soul. Each one precious.

Another thing that can make or break a person's day is what I call elevator relationships. They are relationships that last about as long as a person spends in an elevator. They may happen in a lineup in a store or at a bus stop or in a waiting room. They can bring you up or take you down. You can protect yourself from the down by crossing your arms and covering that tender spot or chakra just below your heart. You can also look away, so you don't absorb their negative energy through your eyes. Just be aware of your own space and keep it private when you need to.

If you look for the small things that give a little happiness to someone else, it will also elevate your spiritual wellbeing. It's the little things that often bring joy to most people in the shortest time.

Sometimes you may be so far down that seeing a way out seems impossible, but it is not. Not unless you decide to remain in your misery, and some people do. The most important thing for yourself to be aware of is not to lose hope. As much as you may be broken, your journey back to health is possible.

Understanding in your heart that you cannot control anyone except yourself is so freeing. Another's journey is theirs and you do not have to concern yourself with anyone else but yourself, and the children you have the privilege to guide to adulthood. We can rarely understand someone else, so let them be. You can still care about them, but leave them to their life as you go on with yours. If they have attacked you and you attack them back, you will both suffer. Where is your healing in that? Be patient with yourself and move on one step at a time. Quietly searching your soul for an answer can be helpful. There are many ways to mend a broken heart. Finding a sacred place and space is helpful in moving forward into healthiness.

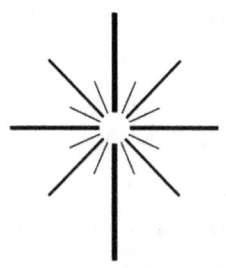

CHAPTER 8

Include all aspects of self in your healing process. Let your spirit help.

We are our own best medicine.

There are many forms of dis-ease which may affect your life and create challenges. Your spiritual self can be your best helper no matter what your condition.

If you are not well in any of the four main aspects of yourself, all are affected. If you are not well physically, your mental, spiritual and emotional are impacted. The same for the others. None are completely independent from the other.

Using spirituality in your healing process can happen in many ways. Your soul is very powerful. So powerful that you can block your own healing if you decide to. If you are going through a challenging time in your life and you get some very confusing, but interesting dreams that you vividly remember, but mean nothing to you on a mental level, it can be your way of working things out on a spiritual level. When this happens, you do not have to worry about how others may interpret these dreams. They may be wrong in their interpretation, maybe not. One thing is for sure. This is your own personal journey, and you can get help from the spirit world whether you are mentally aware of it or not.

Calling on your spiritual helpers, whoever they may be is beneficial. Having a positive attitude toward healing has been proven to help speed the process.

Self-talk is something you can do. Sometimes hearing your own voice formulate possible solutions can be helpful. Whether you are talking to the spirit world or yourself is not important. What matters is that answers come. Never forget that you are who you are, not your condition or situation.

There are helpers who can create a situation where healing can take place. In the case of the physical, a doctor will set bones in such a way they will heal nice and straight. They may prescribe medications which will help with the healing process. They can certainly help develop the situations for the best physical results, but the healing process is yours, and your own spirit can help. In your soul, lies the most powerful strength. The placebo effect is scientific proof that other things besides the physical are at work in the healing process. State of mind and determination also have effect. Some people call on their outer deities for help. There are many ways to communicate in. You can also communicate through thought. Let's not get caught up in the terminology or categorization. It doesn't matter. What matters is that you can ask for help in your own way under the most challenging circumstances you find yourself in.

Whether you use Manitou, God, Allah, Creator, Nature, the Universe or any other word. All the wisdom keepers, no matter their background, say there is only one. There is one for you.

You can evaluate very difficult situations you face, using whatever help is at hand, the wisdom gained may help you see clearly what changes you may need to make. Try to create some balance with an evaluation and appreciation of what you do have. Keeping a balanced approach may open a door to various solutions.

The best solution may be to file things away in what I call the G file. G for garbage. Things that have no purpose in one's present life go in that file. Things that were hurtful in your childhood may still be causing you pain as an adult may need to be dealt with, because it is in your present. With the MeToo movement many people came forward. Bless each and every one for their courage to do so. For others, that may not have been the way to go. Bless them too. In any case do what you need to do conscientiously. Make your journey in the best way possible. Finding your sacred space where you can just BE is a great place to figure out what you need to do. One thing for sure is that if you continue to be bothered, something needs to be sorted out. If you cannot figure it out yourself-seek help. There are people who are trained to deal with issues such as yours. Maybe a family member or friend can help. Keep seeking until you find the helper you need. Be patient with yourself and most importantly, appreciate your journey as you move closer to your wellbeing. In the meantime, take pleasure in all that you do have, even if it is just sunshine and watching nature as it unfolds. Those moments of appreciation are moments of reprieve from your pain. Taking a rest even if it is only for a few moments is still rest. It is good.

If you are in physical danger of being hurt, you may need to formulate an escape route from your situation. An escape route is very freeing whether you use it or not. You know you have given yourself choices should they become necessary. You can use your spiritual knowledge to figure out what works best for you in the moment.

Another great tool in healing is dance. Dance in your own way whenever and wherever you happen to be. Even people who have lost use of some body parts can dance. Many people in wheelchairs dance in their own way as they put their hearts into it. Hospitalized people can dance in their heads. Some people call this freedom dancing or soul dancing. In any case, almost all people throughout the world have some kind of dance they use for healing.

So many things the traditional wisdom keepers know can complement western medicine. A relationship of trust must be built on both sides. That is a big challenge, but the more tools you have for healing the better the chances of the best outcome.

Raven and Dr. Noseworthy, who was the Chief Operational Officer of the Royal Alexandra Hospital in Edmonton, worked collaboratively to complement each medical model. This not only resulted in Native spirituality being brought into the hospital for Native people, but there was a rise of awareness of the needs of other cultures as well.

Spirituality played a big part in traditional healing. Time after time we would see great results when both the western and traditional models would result in the best outcomes. Could that have been because patients felt safer on a spiritual level? Maybe. Could it have been because the people have obtained spiritual help when space was created for that? Likely. Could it be as a result of the respect shown to the Elders? In actuality there could be many reasons, however all we could prove was that outcomes improved. Does it matter why? No, just bask in good results. Know that bringing your spirituality in whichever form it takes can be of great benefit no matter who you are.

A young Native man from the north who had a bad intestinal infection came to the hospital. The doctors could not find a cure for it. No antibiotic seemed to work. He had a big problem with the food. He felt he would die on the diet he was served in the hospital. One weekend we were having a sweat lodge at our place and Raven invited him to attend and he would do prayers for his healing. It took only four days before he was sent back home cured of his stomach ailment. Was it because of the sacred ceremony and prayers, or his inner peace gained from that sacred time with his people, or did the medication suddenly begin to work? Some will think one way and some another. In any case, he got better and that is what was mattered.

Another woman was very ill and the doctor, who was a friend, called the family together and told us that there was nothing more he could do, but if the family wanted to work their magic, go ahead. They did, and the patient got better and went home. She had many more years of good health before she died at a ripe old age.

Another example was our work with diabetes. There was a scientific study proving both short term and long-term success. Each session was started with ceremony asking for help for the people. The western teachings and the traditional teachings worked hand in hand and there is scientific proof that it was more successful for the people than Western medicine on its own. That program is still active today at the Royal Alexandra Hospital in Edmonton.

We, as people, are much more the same than we are different. When it comes to diabetes there is no difference. This program could be easily transferred to any and all peoples. The foundation was to empower the participants to take control of their own condition through understanding what was going on in their body when the sugars went too high or too low. Teachings were done in the form of a sharing circle with a nurse or a dietitian facilitating the teachings to assure that the true facts of diabetes were shared. In sharing, often the people's own experiences was a teaching for everyone. The medical professionals would make sure all the bases of knowledge were covered. Very important was teachings of what symptoms were important to share with their doctors.

For instance, if someone was fatigued a great deal of the time. Rapid weight loss was important as was their thirst pattern. The western medical professionals could be of great help, but they needed the full picture. Participants were also taught how to use both their traditional medicine and the western medicine together. Their well being would not be an either-or situation. Participants were taught how to use both medical models together. With a foundation of understanding and empowering, all tools can work together in harmony. As of yet, there has been none to successfully make the changes needed for the benefit of all people.

Acquiring traditional medicine is approached with reverence. Certain protocol is needed to be followed. The time of year medicines are to be harvested is crucial. The direction they are taken from is most important, and nothing is ever taken without offerings and prayers. There is always reverence for the plants or animals who sacrificed their lives for our benefit. If this knowledge gets lost in our modern world all of mankind will lose. I have hope in that the elders would say "the Creator will never let that happen." So much we understand, so much we don't.

To prove the benefit of certain plants, scientists have taken the plants without protocol. Then they chop them, heat them and break them down into their separate components. Some have been successfully 'discovered.' Even the common aspirin was discovered when science isolated the salicylic acid as the active ingredient of the red willow that rendered the results it has. Many nature people would comment on the fact that side effects are a result of that processing. Some ingredients in the red willow neutralized the negative effects of salicylic acid on its own, so there is a good reason to look at plant medicine in its totality. Maybe science will improve on that too, or maybe not. Because the spiritual aspect of harvesting medicines was not a part of the studies, they were not successful and were therefore discarded as useless.

One interesting development in recent years is that science is catching up to traditional knowledge. There is scientific proof that plants and animals have connections to humans on a spiritual, or energy level, and they often play an important role in our healing journey. This is not new to Nature people. Before contact with Europeans, they thought all people knew. It is common knowledge in their world. So common that they did not understand how others could not know these things.

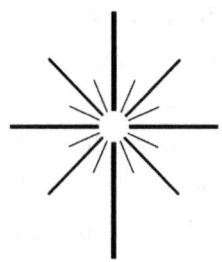

CHAPTER 9

Becoming a Seeker

If you strive for perfection you are guaranteed to fail.
If you strive to do your best, you are guaranteed to succeed

To maneuver through your life journey in a good way, you can go exploring, keeping in mind making your journey just a little better than it was before. Exploring your needs and how to fulfill them is a wonderful journey. Expanding spiritual knowledge takes a desire to learn and the motivation to do the work.

How can you obtain the knowledge you yearn for? Become a seeker. That is how we all learn. We seek the knowledge from those who know.

Many times, Raven and I did workshops with non-native people and Raven always used to say, "You white people have a seed inside of you that is just waiting to grow." Many people's seeds from those interactions did begin to grow. If you like, you too can grow your seed and expand your knowledge to be the best you can be no matter what your circumstances are, who you are or where you reside.

If you want it, go for it.

Seekers of spiritual knowledge are not totally different from seekers of any other kind of knowledge. If you want to specialize in academic knowledge, you become a seeker of academics. We have great institutions of learning. We have places we can go to physically train our bodies if that is our desire and we have fantastic musicians and artists of many sorts. The possibilities are endless. It is all good. We know we will never be all things and only you can choose what is suitable for you. The most important aspect of this is to reject what family, friends and your society think you should be or do. Your decisions are for you alone.

Spiritual wisdom has methods of gathering what you seek which is not always logical to your brain, but don't dismiss it. It may be as valuable to you as brain knowledge. There will be times when things are confusing. Academically there are books written by others which can be referred to, seeking spiritual knowledge there are often no books, no internet, nothing that matches the wisdom keeper's knowledge or the experience you may have in ceremony, prayer or just stillness.

Words are not the only component in spiritual learning. There is also a heart connection. The learning will be confusing at times, especially when you don't get it right away. Raven would say to people who came, "Don't worry. You have asked, so things are in progress. Maybe there is more you need to learn before your question can make sense." Some things will never be suitable to you no matter how many times you hear them. That is the way with all writing, including this one. There is no doubt the writer is sharing his or her truth, but the question to ask yourself 'is it my truth?' Sometimes it is, sometimes it is not. Most important is to remain a free thinker. Free from blind acceptance. Only accept what is right for you. What is universally meant for you.

There is an old saying 'When the pupil is ready the teacher will appear.' The teachers are always there, always ready. When you seek them out and you have a genuine desire to learn they will be there for you. Even the children are your teachers. The wisdom keepers often said to listen to those who have not lost their innocence. That is the children who have not developed filters of what is socially acceptable to talk about, and what is not. In their innocence they only know truth. We can all learn from the innocents. One teaching often shared; the newly arrived on this earth and the those who are ready to end their earth journey close the circle and are the closest to the Creator.

There are millions of stories about universal connections all over the world, of all nations and all genders. Wisdom keepers, from all over the world, who have no physical connection with each other yet talk of similar past powers their ancestors possessed; the ability to levitate, predictions of the future, the use of the same medicines for the same ailments. Surely these similarities cannot all be coincidences.

You can begin your seeking process by using prayer, even if you would not dare say that word. You can simply ask sincerely for answers.

The path to learning is unique to every person. Answers can come through listening to those who know and are doing the work. The first thing is to become aware of yourself, your surroundings, and everything affecting your being. Knowing what you need answers to is definitely helpful, although it may, at times seem confusing. Sometimes you may experience something you know to be special, but if you do not understand it, you can seek out those who know, or you can ignore it.

You can also sleep on it, but before you do, say a little prayer sincerely requesting clarification on what you wish to understand. Who do you pray to? Some call 'IT' God, Allah, Creator, Universe or and many variations of spiritual entities. There are many names, but almost everyone agrees there is only One. One God. One Creator, One Allah, One universe. It comes down to your teachings and your feelings about your teachings. Is everyone fighting about the same thing? What if everyone is right? What if you are manifesting answers from within? Just ask earnestly. You can try. Sometimes there is more to your question than you may realize. Sometimes you will get your answer and not even know when you got it, suddenly you know as surely as the grass is green and water is wet.

There is a very special learning time in the space between when you are asleep and when you are totally relaxed, but not yet in the depth of sleep. Allow your process to happen. The next day you may have some new insight, which could be on a brain level or a spiritual level. In any case, you may know as strongly as you know any other facts in your life. This kind of knowledge will come on its own time, but it will come, and you will know. Trust yourself. There is no need to question.

Always honour your own knowledge. It is passed to you and you alone. The wisdom keepers can help you to understand your experiences and interpret what it might mean for you. If you do not understand what is passed to you, don't worry. Worrying accomplishes nothing.

We have a connection with those in the spirit world. People often came to us who had not grown up with teachings about spirituality yet would often have stories about their ancestors. One woman told us how she often smelled her late father's pipe tobacco. She was not native and did not understand about the connectedness to the spiritual world. We put up a feast and ceremony for her and other non-native people who also experienced connectedness from the spirit world. We all cooked our ancestors' favorite foods including soup for Raven's mom. We smoked the tobacco the woman so often smelled. The connectedness of the spiritual energy could certainly be felt.

Everyone can make a connection. Sincerity is the key. Life is so much easier once you understand that there is help on many levels. The elder's kind of wisdom will take the time it takes, but the learning process is ever so satisfying. I had a friend who wanted things to happen in a hurry. She coined the phrase "Patience is the P word." We often had a good laugh over that.

Sometimes we don't have words. Sometimes words don't matter. Sometimes they do. Sometimes we can't find them.

Never let the lack of words stop your seeking. Categorizing is not necessary. Your feelings are your feelings. What is important is that we seek out ways to consciously do the things that work for our wellbeing. Pay attention to all aspects, including divine influence and celebrate every improvement, everything you learn no matter how small or big. It makes life so much more satisfying for you and all who are in your circle.

You can seek out your wisdom keepers wherever on earth you find them. When you enter other's land be humble and learn the protocol of the territory you enter. Never be afraid to ask for guidance with that. If you become a serious seeker of spiritual knowledge, you have chosen a difficult walk filled with pitfalls. There are true elders in every race, and there are those the late Henry Laboucan from the Lubicon Nation called 'popcorn elders.' How can you distinguish who is who? There are definite signs to watch out for. Some red flags to be wary of is when someone tells you they know how you feel and how to fix you.

No human being can fix another, but they can help.

Those who know, are humble and they quietly go about helping the people. Most important of all in your seeking journey, is to trust yourself in your learning process. If something or someone doesn't feel right to you, it is not. If you discover a situation, you find yourself in, is not for you, just quietly remove yourself.

The elder's teaching was that you 'walk lightly in other's territory'. Referring both to the land, and to the people's ways and beliefs. Listen and learn and be open to their way but never impose yourself in their territory.

By listening and offering their protocol you will learn much. For instance, if you want to learn from a North American Native Elder, you bring tobacco, maybe prayer flags (one or two meters of broadcloth or satin ribbon) and gifts. That can be blankets, or food, or money. In any case you need to find out what their protocol is if you want to learn from them. People who have not bothered may receive nothing, or they may be made a fool of. Seekers need to be humble and listen to whatever teachings are given. If it does not resonate with you right away, then put it aside and let it ruminate until you have a better understanding. That may be a short time, or a long time, or not at all. If you do not get it, it may because it is not meant for you. That is fine. We are all different.

You may lose some people in honoring your spirit, but that's ok. Others will come and stand with you. Does that mean you have to figure things out yourself. Absolutely not. And absolutely yes. Others can help clarify and give you a new insight, but the true knowing comes down to you and you alone. Some will turn to the leaders of their faith group. Some to therapists, family or friends. When you need an answer to your own universal connection keep looking until you are satisfied you have your own. Be prepared that when you receive your answer, you will be going forward with more questions. In the end your connection to Universe is yours and yours alone. Most interesting is that the more you know, the more you know - you don't know. A wonderous thing is knowing that the learning never stops.

Be discerning as to what you share with whom. It can be difficult not to share the things you have become passionate about. Sharing these new insights with people who have not asked for it can create bad feelings and loss of respect. Some people may think you have lost your mind, and nothing is gained but a lot is lost. We all need to take personal freedom no matter what, so if someone does not understand or agree that is their journey. It is ok to differ.

However, the opposite can also happen. There can be a great reward when you bring up a personal spiritual experience, as it may open the door for someone else who is struggling with the understanding of their own journey with spirit. A cautious approach is advisable. Just be prepared to either drop it, or be open to what could turn out to be a very enriching experience with another person. As far as intimate partners are concerned, we need to hook up with people of our own spiritual energy level. Someone to whom you respect and who will respect you and your freedom. Someone you want to cherish as they cherish you. If this has not come your way, you can continue to seek such a relationship if you want. That too is part of seeking. Just enjoy all aspects of your earth journey. Live everyday enjoying your seeking and be grateful you can.

I have been with groups that were so good and so wonderful, and they knew all about spirit and seemed to be so solid in their goodness. Blessings to them in their goodness. My feelings were that I could never be that good, or that confident and so I left and never went back.

There is a group of free spiritual thinkers out of Ft. Saskatchewan who began with just a few like-minded people gathering in one person's home and has since become a much larger gathering of people. Big or small, if you think you would like to share with likeminded people, you could do the exploring to find them, or you could begin your own little group.

Most humans do have a need for tribe, even a small one. The exception being those who decide to live in solitary. Many people will stay with the tribe they were born into. They may feel better with people who speak their language and have the same customs. Most people take pride in where they came from. Expecting others to think like you and believe like you is unrealistic, trying to make others change against their will is disrespectful and hurtful. If you do not respect the land you enter, it is everyone's loss.

What is most important as you wander through life, seek out people your spirit feels most comfortable with. You may stay with them a short time, a long time or a lifetime. If you feel you have outgrown your tribe you may need to move on to another. Honour that. You may need to take some solitary time or if you get a wanderlust, go. All decisions should be about your spiritual wellbeing. Securing stability with a career, a home and putting down roots may be best. Maybe being free of material encumbrances is best. Recognize your present situation and do what is right for you. Your satisfaction is a gift to yourself, your people and the world. Not standing strong on a spiritual level enables others to persuade you to do things you would not otherwise do. Be wary of getting caught up in cults. Seek out those who will guide you to understand your own spiritual experiences.

Throughout the years I spent with the Elders I heard many stories from various people who had special spiritual experiences that made no sense on a mental level, but they did occur nonetheless and the seekers hearts were profoundly touched.

The Elder's response almost always began with 'spiritually passed,' then he or she may proceed to tell the seeker what the message meant. It would depend on whether the seeker had come for the answer or not. Some people had their answers so the Elders would accept whatever their interpretation was. Sometimes they just wanted to be heard. Sometimes when they spoke the answers would come. Sometimes they did need help with interpretation. Often when a person was stuck for words to describe something for which they felt, the elders would finish their thoughts for them, they just knew. Many times, information was passed in the form of a story. That can indeed be confusing. If you get a story which you might think has nothing to do with your answer. It does. Take some time and think about it.

Something else to watch for are messages which come through other people. Someone could be having a normal conversation about anything and then suddenly they will come out with a statement which has nothing to do with the current topic but has everything to do with the issue you are trying to get guidance for. If you ask that person to repeat their conversation, chances are they can't. Therefore, listening carefully will give you answers.

In the realm of spiritual learning there is another space, which is a very important one. If you do not understand what was relayed, but somehow you know in your heart there is something important in it, take the information and put it away. You may create an imaginary bag where you put all those things you cannot immediately process. No worries. There is no pressure to deal with information until the time is right. The knowledge however will be with you at all times, even if it is a mystery. Through the years everything has come out of my bag, but today there is so much more I carry. That's fine. It's not heavy, in fact it is quite nice as I am aware I still have a lot to learn.

We can learn much in the quiet places in nature. When you can sit and just be in the consciousness of the moment, being aware of all that is around you. Prepare to get a teaching. Sometimes your brain is not conscious of what you have learned, but your spirit is. If you want it, it will come. Sometimes in ways that may surprise you, but come it will. Hard to trust for sure, frustrating at times, you bet, will that ever end? Never. When you cross that threshold of knowing that you have learned an important lesson of patience, life gets much easier. As you move on and learn more about WHO you are, life becomes so much easier and satisfying. If we remain open to new knowledge, new ways of learning, the possibilities are endless. It can change your life if you wish.

Wisdom keepers often talked about how we are all connected, whether we are in the physical presence of a person or people, or not. One example almost everyone has experienced is when you are thinking about calling someone on the phone and suddenly, they call you. Sometimes you may have a strong urge to connect with someone whom you are close to. When you do, you may find they are struggling with something which you may be able to help with. Some people have instinctive premonitions and may attempt to warn you of something. Try not to dismiss it if the person is persistent. These are examples of spiritual connection in everyday life.

Many teachers of spiritual knowledge are reluctant to write about these things. They have been known to say that your spirituality does not belong on a flat piece of paper. Therefore, my reluctance in putting this to paper, but I made the decision to do so because we all have spiritual knowledge. Some, like myself before I turned 41, may not have known they have it.

Raven often said, "The road to learning is never ending." I have heard my mother, and many others from all over the world say something similar. That is very comforting as most of us have a love of learning.

I will always be a seeker.

With the lack of understanding between people, there are great challenges to effective communication, but we all laugh the same and cry the same. That we all understand. We are spiritually connected to each other.

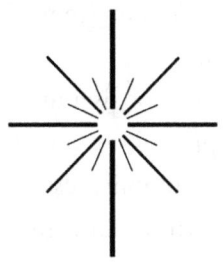

CHAPTER 10

Communication

Communication is likely our number one challenge to achieve harmony.

Lack of meaningful communication between people has caused enormous grief between Nations, relatives and friends. In our western culture, if someone doesn't look you in the eye, it is most often interpreted as that person being untruthful. In the native culture, it's a sign of respect. Some cultures say "lend me your ears, not your eyes."

Communication takes many forms, such as the written and spoken word. There are many other forms of communication. Body language is one, yet it differs greatly between cultures so it can also cause misunderstandings. One effective communication can also be silence.

Truthful communication is important for your spiritual wellbeing. Many people tell lies only to make life less painful for others but then it complicates your life. Truth is always easier in the long run. How many times has the thought 'what am I going to tell him or her' comes into our thoughts. Too often we tell little white lies. These lies hurt us. The problem is not in a little white lie. The problem is with the energy we spend remembering those lies. Remembering truth is much easier.

Gentleness in your honesty is always best. Sometimes no response is necessary. No one needs to explain themselves all the time.

It is always a challenging process to change old habits, but being truthful will give you more peace in your life. When we hide, we are not fully open to receiving messages we may get on a spiritual level.

When people came to Raven for help, it would not take long before they shared if they had spent time in jail or been an alcoholic. They were proud that they had come to a better place and had no need to hide.

Words are so interesting in that they can explain many things, but at the same time, they are ineffective to explain other things. We need to use our own tools to distinguish what words are good for us and which are not.

Here is another dilemma. What a word means to one person may not mean the same to someone else. We are all unique from one culture to another. You, and you alone, are an expert on yourself.

When you set your intention on communicating over vast distances, an effect will occur. Wisdom keepers from all over the world speak of this. Scientists are now 'discovering' it.

People fight hard to retain their language for good reason. Words in any language hold core beliefs of a people. Many times, the wisdom keepers would say that their culture is in the words of their language.

Time and again when the wisdom keepers were communicating in English, which has become the common language between tribes in this part of the world, they would add a word or phrase in their own traditional language which varied by region. Everyone appeared to understand what was meant even when they did not understand the words.

Those who have maintained both their traditional languages, and learned the new languages of the settlers, have wider scope of expressions. Most Native people are eloquent speakers as they use descriptive language.

European languages are stronger in modern concepts. We built big structures, have developed new technologies, to which we have given names. These were not in European traditional languages either, so language becomes fluid in that we make up new words as we go. Native languages tend to lean toward descriptions instead of making up new words. Although we may not always understand one another's knowledge or language, we can still be respectful and remain true to ourselves. One thing we can all do, which is of benefit to the world, is acknowledge each other's unique worldview, language and customs. Life gets so much easier when you stop fighting yourself and others. Easiest is best. A simple nod, a smile, the raising of a hand, a handshake all have a message.

I once belonged to a Spiritual Free Thought group which was comprised of people from various walks of life who wanted to better understand their spiritual selves. One interesting observation was, when someone would struggle to find the right words to express their thoughts or feelings, they would suddenly stop and say, "you know..." Everyone would nod because somehow, we did know. There is a language of the spirit which may not be verbal, but it is understood.

One time when we had a wisdom keeper from Denmark visiting, my Native woman teacher had come to visit us from the north. These people could not understand each other's words, but I understood both languages. When the conversation began, I started to translate, Raven hushed me and said he understood her. I listened to those three sharing about medicines and spiritual connectedness for several hours. Without some kind of universal connection, how could that happen? I don't know, I just know it did. It makes no sense on a mental level, but I know what I saw. I know what I heard.

Some people are either gifted or cursed, whichever way you look at it, with knowing what is going to happen in the future. The fact is they do know.

An example of this is, when my daughter was fourteen years old, she was gifted a horse who she named Sheebe. We went to a local farmer and purchased some hay bales. I found my daughter crying uncontrollably one evening. When I asked her what was wrong, she told me Sheebe was going to die, and she was killing her. I looked out the window and Sheebe was standing quietly in the corral. I knew I had to take her seriously as she'd previously had premonitions that came to pass. I told her we would go to the neighbors, who were horse experts, first thing in the morning and get them over to check things out. When they came, they inspected the hay, and it was full of a deadly mould. If she would have fed it to Sheebe one more day, she would have died.

Time and again I would hear similar stories. Call it intuition, or messages, or whatever you like, but it comes from somewhere. I suspect we all have stories or know someone who has. This is common knowledge to the nature people, so they are not afraid to share their truth amongst themselves. They know they will be believed.

It was always a special moment when a person came and spoke to the wisdom keepers about their encounter with spiritual phenomena and then they discovered they were not losing their minds. Their truth was their truth and there was always a purpose. Sometimes the elders would say 'it was meant to be.' Sometimes, the reason of the vision, would be revealed at a later date.

Many people only saw the truth in that later.

Man has added new concepts through organized religion. Raven often said to those who apologized about their religion. "That is the way you were taught. It's ok" We even had a priest come to some of our ceremonies. Raven always respected everyone's belief system, even when it was not his own. He would remind people that everyone is equal on a spiritual level. Taking mind altering substances such as alcohol and street drugs is not being true to yourself and had no place in his traditional teachings. Some tribes do use hallucinogenic medicines, but they were specific to their ceremonies. They served a specific sacred purpose and were always used in the presence of an elder who could interpret one's visions. No one can tell anyone else when and how to celebrate or expand our spiritual knowledge. We cannot judge another person's journey, only our own. However, the more we understand about someone else, the easier it is to create harmony when we have an open mind.

The circle is a very effective communication tool for respectfully creating understanding between people. In a circle we can all see and hear each other. It is always important to gather as much information as possible for the best decisions to be made for the people the focus is on the person who has the floor. In the circle everyone takes their turn to share beginning with. "I feel, or I think." Everyone will have the opportunity to speak without interruption.

Accusations against anyone are never made, but individuals are free to speak about how they have been personally impacted by a certain incident which may have been created by someone else. For instance: When this action was taken, I felt hurt, or a certain action may have triggered me to respond as I did because.... This creates understanding without an outright accusation. The function of a circle may not be to solve problems. Only to understand them, but in that understanding it is possible to create harmony with or without agreement.

When there are family tensions, it is most important to include everyone, especially the children. Once we understand everyone's point of view, issues are so much easier to solve, taking into account the spiritual feelings of everyone. How do they really feel? What are their concerns? An example of this might be if a family moves from one city to the next; if the children understand the reason for the move, it may make it easier for them to process. Also, if parents know the children's concerns, they can address them before the move. A child, as with adults, need to know what their challenges might be so they can explore the solutions to their fears. One little fellow was deeply concerned about where he would sleep. When the parent assured him that they would take along his bed he felt much better.

Circles are a most useful tool for staff meetings. When the supervisor understands the concerns of their staff, they can efficiently address issues. The goal for a workplace is maximum productivity, so if something stands in the way, those who are closest to the problem often have the best solution. It is well worth a supervisor's time to hear them. If their solutions cannot be addressed, the staff needs to know why. This creates harmony through mutual respect.

If we do not understand other's issues, we cannot always be a part of the solution. When we can do little things for one another, everyone gains.

Because many things cannot be proven scientifically, for some people it can never be true. You may argue about the difference between spirit and emotion. It matters not what words you use for your journey. What matters is the journey itself. Words are limiting and spiritual knowledge is not.

Another dilemma is how would you know if someone else's perception is the same as yours? For instance, how do you know if someone else sees color the way you do? How can you describe colour without comparing. We use blue as...green as...red as..., etc. Even in that comparison one person sees color differently from another person.

Communication on a spiritual level is even more individual, and will vary greatly from one person to another.

For instance, wisdom keepers couldn't tell anyone what they would experience when entering a sweat lodge, or attending a ceremony. Some people were accustomed to having expectancies laid out in advance. It can indeed be frustrating until one learns to let go of expectations and accept what came, if anything. The elders are always there to help make sense of whatever happens. Sometimes if people did not understand their answers, elders would say "Don't worry, you will get your answers to what you have asked." They may come in a dream, or people will be a conduit between the spirit world and yourself. Sometimes, if you are having a conversation with someone about a totally different topic then they make a statement which makes no sense in the context of your conversation, but is the answer to what you were seeking. This is magic, or is it?

One day you may also look back and realize that you have your answer. You know you have had it for a while, but when it happened and how, may be a mystery to you. It just is.

Spirit communicates in its own unique way.

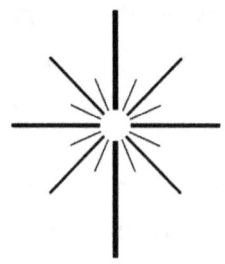

CHAPTER 11

Judging

When someone does you wrong, they will suffer karma. If you retaliate with hateful revenge, you too will suffer karma. No one wins.

Putting judgement on yourself, or another person accomplishes nothing. Never compare yourself with anyone else. Knowing WHO you are and accepting yourself, with your limitations and your dreams, and all that is you, will bring you the most satisfaction possible. Elders were always accepting of everyone. In fact, some people who are man/woman were greatly respected as they have a special understanding of people which may illude others. The same for some people who have been diagnosed with autism. They most often possess a special gift of perception the average person does not. Their gifts should not go unrecognized. Sometimes people have unrealistic expectations of others.

Just accept others as they are, without question, rather than what you would like them to be.

Take Michener Center in Red Deer, Alberta. It was a center where 1600 mentally and physically handicapped people lived, they too were my teachers. A young lad in his early 20s bragged so proudly of how he had dressed himself for the very first time. He accomplished everything we all strive for, complete and utter happiness! The joy for his great accomplishment was evident, not only in his words, but also in his actions. He jumped up and down with glee and hugged and kissed everyone around him that allowed it. He was WHO he was. He was one of my teachers about how judging one's accomplishments against another is unrealistic. He loved the best he could as did every one of the 1600 people who lived there.

Pain cannot be compared from one person to another person. Pain is pain, degree comparison is unrealistic. We make what we consider mistakes in our lives. Everyone has. Remember that you can only make decisions within the conditions that exist in the present and hindsight is 20/20 vision. Therefore, it may not have been a mistake at the time. Judging by the present life situation can be very damaging. Most people do their best with where they are at in life.

Looking at one's life in an honest manner, without interpretation, without judgement, will create the most harmony possible in your present. It may take some practice to keep judgement out, some do have challenging parenting skills. It is what it is. Single parents who work two or three jobs just to keep food on the table and give their children a safe place to live are especially vulnerable to self judgement. If a child goes awry as an adult, parents will often blame themselves and their decisions. Often an adult child will also blame a parent. In actuality that is sometimes just an excuse for their bad behavior, and it is giving them a free pass in their own minds. Adults, including your adult children, make their own decisions.

There is help for those who want to change. Too many people get in their own way. Some decide to live in their misery. Elders knew that if a person was not ready to do their own healing it would never happen. You cannot fix anyone else, but you can help. It does take a great deal of power to climb out of a miserable hole. Some never make it. Those who do have earned the greatest respect. Elders never judged anyone. They were always there and seizing the opportunity to help when the time was right. No one came to seek help from Raven unless they were straight and sober for four days. That was protocol. When they did come, it didn't matter what a person had done in the past, they were accepted and respected for seeking help.

Once a fellow came to see Raven, this person had just been released from prison for doing terrible things to a little girl some thirty years earlier. I knew the story well from the news reports so long ago. Raven was asked to do a sweat lodge for this man, and he agreed. The day came and a car pulled up. Three men got out and there was no way to tell which one was the 'bad guy' until we were introduced. The sweat happened and afterwards everyone there shook the man's hand and thanked him. In my confusion I asked Raven why they would thank someone who had done something so evil. He looked at me in surprise and said simply "He came here to heal himself." For that everyone was grateful.

Basic understanding among elders is that no person is evil, even though what they have done may be evil. It was recognized that you are not what you do. You are who you are. Therefore, there was always hope for healing. When someone had been in jail, on the streets, drug and alcohol addicted, but were now clean, they were proud of their accomplishment, and people were proud to talk about it. That was a good lesson in common sense. Why shouldn't they be proud? They too lived the best they could at any one time.

No one truly knows about the core, or soul of another person, but the elders always knew whether a person was sincere or not. You can only live your own life. Does that mean you have to be selfish? Yes!! If you are spiritually strong and healthy, you will know whether to help someone or let them go. They may be loving the best they can, but it may not be healthy for you to be in their presence, so bless them over there, away from you, knowing they may be toxic to you at this time.

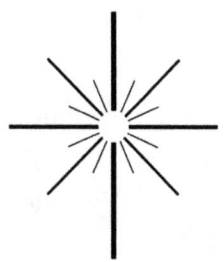

CHAPTER 12

Live Life in the Moment.

Plan on having the best day possible, the best hour possible, the best minute possible and it will culminate in the best life possible.

This poem I wrote at a time when I knew there were people who were wanting to kill me and I did not know if I would have more than that very moment. Looking back, it has been a gift. I learned so much about the value of NOW and living life for the present.

LIFE IN THE MOMENT

Life in the moment is a clear blue sky,
The sun the color of gold.
Life in the moment doesn't wonder why
It helps to keep a hold.

Life in the moment is grass so green,
The bugs that call it home.
Life in the moment is being seen,
Is having the courage to roam.

Life in the moment is a gentle rain
That cleanses the beautiful land.
Life in the moment is relief from pain,
Relief that gives us a hand.

Life in the moment is the sky at night,
The stars that twinkle so.
Life in the moment is rays of light
Allowing our spirits to grow.

Life in the moment is snow on the trees,
The frost you see with the cold.
Life in the moment allows you to be
Just who you are, young or old.

Life in the moment is the powerful sea,
The waves that come and go.
Life in the moment is being me,
Allowing myself to grow.

Life in the moment is all that is real,
So make it all it can be.
Life in the moment is what you feel
So look at yourself and see.

Being aware of your thought pattern is important to your spiritual health. Pay attention to your feelings as they present themselves in the moment and remember to look for the humour in every situation.

When you need to make difficult choices, think about the consequences of each choice. Ask yourself how you feel when making one decision, or the other. The why doesn't matter. When you go to how you feel about your choice, your decision becomes clearer. Take the time it takes. When you have even small frustrations in your life, take the time to figure out a way to ease them. For instance, if you get really annoyed, with even the little things like losing your keys, maybe you can hang them on the doorknob. Putting a key hanger close to the door might be a solution. Being conscious of the little things that are annoying you and work to change them is good for your spirit.

If you worry about bills, set up a system that works for you. Maybe you can pay them as soon as they arrive. Maybe you can put them away and pay them all at once at the most convenient time. In any case whatever is annoying for you, explore how you can improve your situation without judgement no matter how small or big. Once you know who you are, these changes will be made from a place of strength. Maybe not in the eyes of someone else, but once you figure yourself out, you stop caring about what others think of you. Live your life in ways that work for you.

Making a conscious effort to live life without judgment will have great payoffs. Live in as much harmony as possible in the present, knowing that the past cannot be changed.

If a mistake has been made, don't waste your time figuring out who made the mistake, unless it is necessary to fix it for the present or future. For instance, if there is a mix-up in an appointment, the important thing is to get another appointment, not who made the mistake. If an object is not brought to a certain place, and two people thought the other was taking it, it is not important who was to bring it to whom. The important thing is that the object is brought to where it needs to go. Spending time trying to find fault for the sake of fault can too often lead to unnecessary disharmony. Just look for solutions that will result in the most harmonious outcomes.

If there is conflict with another person in your life, the first questions to ask yourself are; Will it matter tomorrow if you are miserable? Is it really your business? How is your misery benefiting you? What needs to be done to improve your situation? Can anything really improve? If you cannot, maybe you can file your issues, so it is not a part of your everyday. Maybe you just need to accept your situation and make the best of it, which may include simply staying away from certain people or situations. Make every moment the best it can be. you can't do better.

When I was going through an especially challenging time in my life and I spent time in the depth of despair, I would occasionally ask myself if this pity party for one had gone on long enough. Most of the time I found humour in that statement, but once in a while I would say no. Then I would just stay in my misery a little while longer, but with that sentence I became aware of the need to move on. You too can find a way that works for your own spiritual wellbeing.

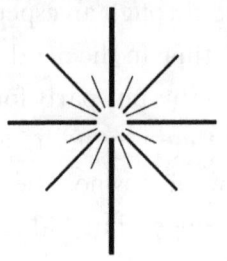

CHAPTER 13

It's Your Life Journey

Make your life journey the best you can in every way possible, remain true to yourself in all your challenges.

Live your life on your own terms to the best of your ability. Never strive to be anything you are not. It is your life, live it consciously in your own way. Never make promises you can't fulfill. Never, ever compromise yourself.

Always be aware of what and who will bring you the most satisfaction in your present situation. You will have conflict at times, which will cause disharmony, but your aim should not be to place blame, but to do a thorough evaluation to figure out what action you may need to take to bring back harmony.

Live life being grateful for what you have and don't give much thought to what you do not have. If you have enough to eat, a warm bed to sleep in, and clothes on your body, you have more than many. Be grateful. Bringing gratitude into your life will help to lift your spirit. Everyone has things to be grateful for. A good night's sleep, a nice sunny day, the rain so plants can grow, and we can eat. Being able to purchase groceries you need is another thing to be grateful for. If you are short of funds, look for bargains and appreciate the savings. Food banks are there to help you through an emergency.

Everyone has something to be grateful for. Some homeless people are ever so grateful for a community that cares about one another. Satisfaction is found in so many places and situations in our everyday lives, no matter how humble our circumstances. Find free events to go to. Spend time with those you love. When you overcome challenges, no matter how small, be grateful. Being grateful fills your thoughts with good things for the soul. You cannot be miserable and grateful at the same time.

Never put clothing on your body you don't like. That is hard on your spiritual self. Owning only a few items is fine as long as putting them on makes you feel good. There are so many things you can do which does not require a great deal of revenue.

Sleeping in a hammock outside to sky-watch is great for some. Smells of nature and the peace of taking a break from the mechanical noises of machines, the refrigerator turning on and off might be a welcomed change.

Sitting out in nature in the rain and focusing on the sounds is good for the soul. Laying on your belly, observing and concentrating on a very small square of land you may find all kinds of interesting living beings in your chosen place. Lying on Mother Earth and asking her to share her energy is healing. Going on a nature walk, becoming conscious of all you see is a good healing tool. The important thing is to find what works for you in the moment.

When you do these things, does that mean you are too selfish? No. Most of us inherently like to be helpful and please others, but if we are not the best we can be, that can be challenging.

When life gets overwhelming, think about what you can eliminate. Are you too involved with things that are none of your business? Walk away. Which of your chores can wait?

Figure out a way to do what you love, and it will bring in the money. If you love to teach, someone will pay you to do that. If you love to argue, become a lawyer. No matter what, look for what you love to do, and the money does follow and your spirit will be happy. If you cannot find something you like to do, but need the money now, just do what you need to do temporarily, keeping in mind that there is most likely a way to your goal. If not, you may need to accept that too.

Living life in the present will minimize stress about the future. That does not mean you do not make plans for your future. We all have vision for what may lie ahead. For instance, if you want to start your own business, figure out what needs to be done today. What information needs to be collected, what type of facility do you need, what equipment do you need and where can it come from. Just tackle the least number of issues at one time. That will make the present easier to handle. Then you are planning for success, and your spirit won't get too overwhelmed. Don't stress out about unpacking boxes after a move. Take a rest, the boxes will still be there when you get up. Don't worry. Worry is probably the biggest drainer of your spiritual energy and it accomplishes nothing.

Every life journey is a roller coaster ride with ups and downs along the way. You will learn, and grow from the downs too, they are important.

Even if you are lucky enough to have an abundance of money, it does not preclude you are happy with your lot in life. Keep an open mind as to where you want to head in the next leg of your journey. Maybe you do not want to learn any more for a while. If you're tired, take a rest.

Explore new thoughts, new adventures for as long as you wish. There may come a time when you just want to be still and enjoy where you are in the moment. If you have lived your life fully, you will have an abundance of good memories. You will also carry bad memories, but you do not have to make them a part of your everyday life. You can still appreciate becoming a wiser person because of them.

My hope and prayer for you is to have the best earth journey possible.

Epilogue

Everything I put to paper is the absolute truth, but it is my truth.

Some parts will be suitable to you, some won't. Therefore, I would ask you to take from this writing what resonates with you and leave the rest on the pages of this book.

There is not one statement I make in this book that cannot be argued and rightfully so. We all have our own unique spiritual journey. Nothing is for everyone. When you celebrate yours, the best you can, under whatever circumstances you face, that is success. My hope is that some of what I shared may be helpful in making your best earth journey possible. That is what I learned from the Native people, they gifted me, with an understanding of spirit and making humour a part of my life.

I will be forever grateful to the wisdom keepers for their teachings. They guided me to be a free thinker and from them I gained a pathway to personal freedom.

Hai Hai. Ish Nish, Mahsi Cho, Merci Beaucoup, Tak and Thank you.

Other Books
by Rita Makkannaw

Journeys with Raven

Two Worlds Together

From Smoke Signals to Cell Phones

I am White: Eagle Woman Flies with Raven

Thank you for completing *Wandering Wisely In Balance*.

We would love if you could help by posting a review at your book retailer and on the PageMaster Publishing site. It only takes a minute and it would really help others by giving them an idea of your experience.

Thanks

PM Store Author's QR Code
https://pagemasterpublishing.ca/by/Rita-Makkannaw/

To order more copies of this book, find books by other Canadian authors, or make inquiries about publishing your own book, contact PageMaster at:

PageMaster Publication Services Inc.
11340-120 Street, Edmonton, AB T5G 0W5
books@pagemaster.ca
780-425-9303

catalogue and e-commerce store
PageMasterPublishing.ca/Shop

www.ingramcontent.com/pod-product-compliance
Lightning Source LLC
LaVergne TN
LVHW051510070426
835507LV00022B/3028